H

Delicious and Nutritious Snack Recipes

By: **Celeste Jarabese**

Table of Contents

Introduction

This book provides you with snack recipes that are easy to make and uses healthy ingredients.

Snacks are small meals in-between the 3 main meals namely – Breakfast, Lunch, and Dinner. Snacking is very important because it can help you in replenishing your body with essential nutrients for a more stable source of energy until your next meal.

Ideally, snacks are light meals that provide one-fourth of your daily calories to let your body stave off hunger until you have your next meal. Eating healthy snacks also discourages the urge to binge eat. Binge eating is an eating disorder that can easily lead to undesirable weight gain.

With the current aggressive marketing of snack products like chips, sodas, and other foods that are filled with trans-fats and sugars, snacking has become one of the major causes of weight gain. Thus, promoting obesity along with the risks that come with it.

Meal planning is essential to have well-balanced meals daily. Choosing the right foods to eat especially during snack time is equally important so that you will be rewarded with a healthy body and sound mind.

Healthy snacks can provide you with foods high in fiber, vitamins, minerals, and antioxidants. These are very important components in making sure that your body organs are working well.

In this book, you will find snack recipes that consist of nutrient-dense ingredients like fresh fruits and vegetables, dairies, cereals, seeds, and nuts. With this, you can improve your snack choices and consume only healthy foods that promote wellness.

This book offers a wide selection of recipes from vegetable sticks with scrumptious dips to delicious and healthy cookies to salads and revitalizing drinks. I hope you'll enjoy all of them!

Tips for Choosing the Right Ingredients for Your Healthy Snack

With the different kinds of ingredients available in the market today, from fresh to processed foods, it is a bit tricky to maneuver your way into choosing and buying nutritious and healthy ingredients. So here are a few tips to guide you in selecting the right ingredients for your healthy snacks!

1. *Choose snack ingredients that are included under the healthy food groups.*

   When choosing your snack, it is best to concentrate on these food groups - fruits, vegetables, whole grains, lean protein sources, dairy products, seeds, and nuts. These foods should be used as main ingredients in making your snack instead of high caloric foods that contain a low nutritive value.

2. *Substitute high sugar and high-fat food items with healthier alternatives.*

   Instead of making use of ingredients that are high in sugar and fat, you can substitute them with healthier choices like wholegrain cereals, low-fat or fat-free dairies, raw sugar or honey, lean cuts of meat, and the use of olive oil in making salad dressings.

3. *Use herbs and spices as flavor enhancers, rather than salt or MSG.*

   A high consumption of salt or MSG-laden foods increases the chance of acquiring health issues, so instead of using the conventional salt and MSG to enhance the flavor of your food, you can use herbs and spices instead. It will also bring out a more natural flavor of the food.

4. *Buy fresh versions of food or make them from scratch at home, instead of purchasing processed or ready-made ingredients.*

   Processed and commercially manufactured ingredients are usually high in sodium content and fats, especially trans-fat and saturated fat, which is why it is better to prepare your snacks from fresh ingredients to minimize the consumption of unhealthy ingredients that may contribute to health risks.

5. *Keep nutritious and healthy snack choices easily available.*

   Researches show that food availability affects your snack choices. For example, if your cupboard at home is filled with chips, sodas, and candies they can easily be your snack anytime you feel the need to have one. But if you have fruits, vegetables, seeds, and nuts in your refrigerator or pantry, it will be easier for you to have the right choice of snack.

Just follow these guidelines, and you will be on your way to preparing your very own healthy snack!

Cucumber and Carrot Sticks with Ranch Dip

Preparation Time: 10 minutes
Total Time: 20 minutes
Yield: 5 servings

Ingredients

2 medium cucumber, cut into 3-inch sticks (400 g)
3 medium carrots, cut into 3-inch sticks (180 g)

Ranch Dip:
1/2 cup light mayonnaise (125 g)
3 Tbsp. buttermilk (45 ml)
1 clove garlic, minced (3 g)
1 Tbsp. fresh parsley, chopped (3.5 g)
1 Tbsp. chives, chopped (3.5 g)
kosher salt and freshly ground black pepper

Method

1. In a small mixing bowl, whisk together mayonnaise, buttermilk, garlic, parsley, and chives. Mix thoroughly and keep in the refrigerator until ready to use.
2. Arrange cucumber and carrots sticks in individual serving cups.
3. Take out chilled ranch dip, and transfer in a serving bowl. Garnish with parsley.
4. Serve and enjoy.

Nutritional Information:

Energy - 125 kcal, Fat - 8.1 g, Carbs - 13.1 g, Protein - 1.6 g, Sodium - 213 mg

Garden Salad with Strawberry Vinaigrette

Preparation Time: 20 minutes
Total Time: 20 minutes
Yield: 4 servings

Ingredients
2 medium cucumber, diced (400 g)
2 medium tomatoes, diced (250 g)
6 oz. feta cheese (180 g)
1 small head Romaine lettuce (350 g)

Strawberry Vinaigrette
2 Tbsp. strawberry puree (30 g)
2 Tbsp. balsamic vinegar (30 ml)
1 Tbsp. honey (20 ml)
1/4 cup extra-virgin olive oil (60 ml)
salt and pepper, to taste

Method
1. Make the dressing by placing the strawberry puree in a small bowl. Whisk in vinegar, honey, and olive oil. Stir well. Season with salt and pepper. Set aside.
2. Toss together cucumber, tomatoes and feta cheese in a medium bowl. Place salad over a bed of lettuce.
3. Drizzle strawberry vinaigrette over salad.
4. Serve and enjoy.

Nutritional Information:
Energy - 190 kcal, Fat - 14.2 g, Carbs - 13.1 g, Protein - 5.1 g, Sodium - 294 mg

Homemade Garden Salad

Preparation Time: 15 minutes
Total Time: 20 minutes
Yield: 4 servings

Ingredients

1 small head Romaine lettuce (350 g)
2 medium tomatoes, diced (250 g)
1/2 medium cucumber, sliced thinly (100 g)
2 oz. black olives, whole (60 g)
4.5 oz. feta cheese, cubed (130 g)

Red Wine Vinaigrette Dressing
1/4 cup extra-virgin olive oil (60 ml)
2 Tbsp. red wine vinegar (30 ml)
1 Tbsp. Dijon mustard (15 g)
pinch salt
pinch black ground pepper

Method

1. Make the dressing first by mixing all the ingredients together in a small bowl. Set aside.
2. Cut the Romaine lettuce into small bite-sized pieces.
3. In a salad bowl, combine in all vegetables. Top with feta cheese.
4. Serve with vinaigrette dressing on the side.

Nutritional Information:

Energy - 223 kcal, Fat - 19.3 g, Carbs - 6.8 g, Protein - 5.2 g, Sodium - 394 mg

Mango and Cherry Tomato Salad

Preparation Time: 10 minutes
Total Time: 10 minutes
Yield: 4 servings

Ingredients
10 oz. arugula or baby rocket (300 g)
2 cups grape tomatoes, whole (300 g)
1 cup ripe mango, cubed (165 g)
2 Tbsp. capers, rinsed and drained (30 g)

Apple Cider Vinaigrette Dressing:
1 Tbsp. Dijon mustard (15 g)
1 clove garlic, minced (3 g)
3 Tbsp. apple cider vinegar (45 ml)
1/4 cup extra-virgin olive oil (60 ml)
Kosher salt and pepper, to taste

Method
1. Make the dressing by combining all the dressing ingredients together. Set aside until ready to serve.
2. Mix arugula, grape tomatoes, mangos, and capers together in a large salad bowl. Divide among 4 individual plates.
3. Serve with dressing on the side.
4. Enjoy.

Nutritional Information:
Energy - 199 kcal, Fat - 13.8 g, Carbs - 19.4 g, Protein - 3.6 g, Sodium - 197 mg

Easy Egg and Tomato Salad

Preparation Time: 15 minutes
Total Time: 15 minutes
Yield: 4 servings

Ingredients

10 oz. arugula leaves or baby rocket (300 g)
1 medium cucumber, sliced (200 g)
1 1/2 cups cherry tomatoes, halved (225 g)
4 (2 oz. or 60 g) medium hard-boiled eggs

Garlic Balsamic Mustard Dressing
3 Tbsp. balsamic vinegar (45 ml)
1 Tbsp. Dijon mustard (15 g)
1 clove garlic, minced (3 g)
1/4 cup extra-virgin olive oil (60 ml)
Kosher salt and pepper, to taste

Method

1. First, make the Balsamic Vinaigrette by combining all the dressing ingredients together. Set aside.
2. In a salad bowl, mix together arugula, cucumber and tomatoes.
3. Slice the boiled eggs vertically to make 8 slices per egg.
4. Divide salad in individual plates and top with sliced eggs.
5. Serve with dressing on side.

Nutritional Information:
Energy - 218 kcal, Fat - 17.7 g, Carbs - 7.6 g, Protein - 8.2 g, Sodium - 276 mg

Beet Cucumber and Tomato Salad

Preparation Time: 15 minutes
Total Time: 30 minutes
Yield: 4 servings

Ingredients

1 lb. beets, washed and peeled (450 g)
1 lb. cucumber, sliced thinly (450 g)
1 cup grape or cherry tomatoes, halved (150 g)

Honey Mustard Vinegar Dressing:
1 Tbsp. honey (20 g)
1 Tbsp. Dijon mustard (15 g)
2 Tbsp. lemon juice (30 ml)
1/4 cup extra-virgin olive oil (60 ml)
Kosher salt and pepper, to taste

Method

1. Cut peeled beets into thin sliced.
2. In a salad bowl, mix together beets, cucumber, cherry tomatoes and onions.
3. Whisk together honey, lemon juice, and Dijon mustard. Blend well. Gradually stir in olive oil. Season with salt and pepper. Set aside.
4. Serve vegetables in a serving bowl and drizzle dressing on top.

Nutritional Information:

Energy - 215 kcal, Fat - 13.2 g, Carbs - 24.4 g, Protein - 3.5 g, Sodium - 285 mg

Radish Cucumber and Herb Salad

Preparation Time: 15 minutes
Total Time: 15 minutes
Yield: 4 servings

Ingredients
1 medium cucumber, sliced into thin half-moons (200 g)
3 cups radish, sliced thinly (360 g)
1/4 cup spring onion, chopped (15 g)
1/4 cup fresh parsley leaves (15 g)
sea salt and pepper, to taste

Lemon Dressing
1 small shallot, thinly sliced (40 g)
1 zest of lemon (3.5 g)
2 Tbsp. lemon juice (30 ml)
1/4 cup extra-virgin olive oil (60 ml)

Method
1. Make the dressing by whisking together the shallots, lemon zest and lemon juice. Stand for about 3 minutes. Then gradually whisk in olive oil.
2. In a large mixing bowl, combine together cucumber, radishes, spring onion, and parsley.
3. Drizzle with dressing. Toss to coat. Season with salt and pepper.
4. Serve and enjoy.

Nutritional Information:
Energy - 137 kcal, Fat - 12.8 g, Carbs - 6.6 g, Protein - 1.1 g, Sodium - 158 mg

Homemade Kale Chips

Preparation Time: 25 minutes
Total Time: 45 minutes
Yield: 8 servings

Ingredients

4.4 lbs. kale, washed and dried (2 kg)
4 Tbsp. olive oil (60 ml)
lemon pepper, to taste
garlic powder, to taste

Method

1. Preheat oven at 275 F.
2. Remove tough kale stems and cut leaves into 1 ½ - inches. Set aside in a bowl.
3. Drizzle olive oil and sprinkle lemon pepper and garlic powder over kale. Toss to coat evenly.
4. Arrange kale in baking sheet, making sure there are no overlapping leaves. Bake in batches if needed.
5. Bake for 20 minutes turning the leaves halfway through until crispy.
6. Serve and enjoy.

Nutritional Information:

Energy - 137 kcal, Fat - 5.6 g, Carbs - 19.0 g, Protein - 5.4 g, Sodium - 195 mg

Carrots and Peas with Herbed Sour Cream

Yogurt Dip

Preparation Time: 15 minutes
Total Time: 15 minutes
Yield: 4 servings

Ingredients
1 lb. baby carrots, cleaned (450 g)
1 lb. snow peas, cleaned and trimmed (450 g)

Herbed Yogurt Dip
3/4 cup plain Greek yogurt (180 g)
1 Tbsp. minced green onion, white and light green parts only (3.5 g)
1 Tbsp. finely chopped flat-leaf parsley (3.5 g)
1 Tbsp. sherry vinegar (15 ml)
Himalayan salt and pepper, to taste

Method
1. In a mixing bowl, combine together the dip ingredients. Mix well and cover with cling wrap and refrigerate until ready to serve.
2. Arrange carrots and snow peas in a serving plate and serve with chilled herbed sour cream yogurt dip.

Nutritional Information:
Energy - 120 kcal, Fat - 1.3 g, Carbs - 19.2 g, Protein - 8.8 g, Sodium - 255 mg

Vegetable Sticks with Spiced Yogurt Dip

Preparation Time: 15 minutes
Total Time: 15 minutes
Yield: 4 servings

Ingredients
2 celery stalks, cut into 3 inch sticks (120 g)
1 medium cucumber, cut into 3 inch sticks (200 g)
2 medium carrot, cut into 3 inch sticks (120 g)
1 medium red bell pepper, deseeded and sliced into sticks
(120 g)

Spiced Yogurt Dip
1 cup plain Greek yogurt (250 g)

1 Tbsp. fresh lime juice (15 ml)

1 tsp. honey (7 ml)

1/2 tsp. sweet paprika, ground (1 g)

1/2 tsp. cumin, ground (1 g)

Himalayan salt and pepper, to taste

Method
1. In a medium bowl, mix together yogurt, lime juice,
   honey, paprika, and cumin. Season to taste.
2. Serve vegetable sticks with spiced yogurt dip on side.
3. Enjoy.

Nutritional Information:

Energy - 91 kcal, Fat - 1.5 g, Carbs - 13.6 g, Protein - 7.2 g, Sodium - 196 mg

Olive Tomato and Feta Mini Skewers

Preparation Time: 10 minutes
Total Time: 10 minutes
Yield: 24 servings

Ingredients
2 cups cherry tomatoes, halved (300 g)
8 oz. feta cheese, diced (250 g)
24 black olives, pitted (8 g)
24 decorative skewers or toothpicks

Method
1. Thread olives, cherry tomatoes, and feta cheese onto the skewers or toothpicks. Place in a serving dish.
2. Serve and enjoy.

Nutritional Information:

Energy - 33 kcal, Fat - 2.5 g, Carbs - 1.2 g, Protein - 1.5 g, Sodium - 125 mg

Shrimp and Cottage Cheese on Cucumber Cups

Preparation time: 20 minutes
Total time: 20 minutes
Yield: 12 servings

Ingredients
4 (200 g) cucumbers
1 lb. (450 g) medium shrimps, cooked, peeled and deveined
2 tablespoons (30 ml) olive oil
1 tablespoon (15 ml) lime juice
1/2 teaspoon (1 g) dried parsley
6 oz. (180 g) cottage cheese
1/4 cup (60 g) light mayonnaise
1 (3 g) clove garlic, minced
1/2 teaspoon (1 g) coriander seed, ground
salt and freshly ground black pepper

Method
1. Using a knife or peeler, score the length of each cucumber alternately. Trim the ends and cut crosswise to make 4 pieces. Scoop out the seeds, leaving some at the bottom to hold the filling. Set aside.
2. In a medium bowl, mix together olive oil, lime juice, and parsley. Add the shrimps and toss to coat. Season with salt and pepper, to taste. Let sit for a few minutes.
3. Meanwhile, combine the cottage cheese, mayonnaise, garlic, and coriander in a small bowl. Season with salt and pepper. Mix well. Transfer into a piping or pastry bag with star tip.

4. Pipe the cottage cheese filling onto the center of each cucumber cup. Top individually with shrimp. Place in a serving dish.
5. Serve and enjoy.

Nutritional Information:

Energy - 129 kcal, Fat - 9.4 g, Carbs - 5.7 g, Protein - 6.5 g, Sodium - 180 mg

Mini Kiwi and Cheese Skewers

Preparation time: 15 minutes
Total time: 15 minutes
Yield: 12 servings

Ingredients

4 (85 g) kiwifruit, peeled
4 oz. (125 g) cheddar cheese
4 oz. (125 g) mozzarella cheese
toothpicks or decorative mini skewers

Method

1. Cut the kiwi, cheddar, and mozzarella cheese into small squares.
2. Thread the kiwi alternately with the cheese onto each toothpick or small skewer.
3. Arrange the mini skewers in a serving platter.
4. Serve and enjoy.

Nutritional Information:

Energy - 80 kcal, Fat - 4.9 g, Carbs - 4.2 g, Protein - 5.3 g, Sodium - 116 mg

Marinated Balsamic Mozzarella Sticks

Preparation Time: 15 minutes
Total Time: 1 hour 15 minutes
Yield: 4 servings

Ingredients

1 lb. mozzarella, cut into 3-inch sticks (450 g)

Balsamic Marinade
1/4 cup extra-virgin olive oil (60 ml)
1/4 cup balsamic vinegar (60 ml)
1 clove garlic, minced (3 g)
1 tsp. Italian seasoning (2 g)
Himalayan salt and pepper, to taste

Method

1. Make the marinade by whisking the olive oil, balsamic vinegar, garlic, Italian seasoning together in a small bowl. Season with salt and pepper.
2. Pour balsamic marinate over the mozzarella sticks, making sure each mozzarella is evenly covered.
3. Chill in refrigerator for about at least 1 hour.
4. Take it out from the refrigerator and serve.

Nutritional Information:

Energy - 142 kcal, Fat - 12.8 g, Carbs - 1.3 g, Protein - 6.0 g, Sodium - 129 mg

Herbed Cottage Cheese on Whole Wheat

Crackers

Preparation Time: 10 minutes
Total Time: 10 minutes
Yield: 5 servings

Ingredients
20 pcs. crackers of your choice, preferably whole-wheat

Herbed Cottage Cheese
6 oz. cottage cheese (180 g)
6 oz. sour cream (180 g)
1 Tbsp. shallot, minced (10 g)
1 Tbsp. green onion, minced (3.5 g)
1 Tbsp. parsley, minced (3.5 g)
lemon pepper, to taste

Method
1. In a small bowl, whisk together cottage cheese, sour cream, shallot, green onion, and parsley. Season with lemon pepper.
2. Cover with cling wrap and chill in the refrigerator until ready to serve.
3. Serve with crackers. Garnish with parsley, if desired.
4. Enjoy.

Nutritional Information:
Energy - 147 kcal, Fat - 5.3 g, Carbs - 14.3 g, Protein - 9.5 g, Sodium - 344 mg

Fresh Tomato and Herb Bruschetta

Preparation Time: 15 minutes
Total Time: 15 minutes
Yield: 10 servings

Ingredients

1 (8 oz. or 250 g) wholegrain baguette, sliced into 1-inch thick
3 medium tomatoes, diced (375 g)
1/4 cup fresh basil, chopped (15 g)
2 Tbsp. fresh thyme, chopped (7 g)
1 clove garlic, minced (3 g)
3 Tbsp. extra virgin olive oil (45 ml)
2 Tbsp. balsamic vinegar (30 ml)
Kosher salt and pepper, to taste
Fresh basil leaves, for garnish

Method

1. In a medium bowl, combine together tomatoes, basil, thyme, and garlic. Drizzle with olive oil and balsamic vinegar. Toss to coat well. Season to taste.
2. Toast baguette slices in a broiler for about 1-2 minutes.
3. Use a dessert spoon to scoop the tomato mixture over the toasted bread and place on a serving dish. Garnish with fresh basil.
4. Serve and enjoy.

Nutritional Information:

Energy - 145 kcal, Fat - 4.9 g, Carbs - 21.4 g, Protein - 4.5 g, Sodium - 288 mg

Tomato Feta and Basil Bruschetta

Preparation Time: 15 minutes
Total Time: 15 minutes
Yield: 10 servings

Ingredients

1 (8 oz. or 250 g) wholegrain baguette, sliced into 1-inch thick
2 cups cherry tomatoes, sliced into quarters (300 g)
1/2 medium zucchini, sliced into thin half circles (100 g)
2 Tbsp. fresh basil, basil (7 g)
1 small red onion, sliced into strips (90 g)
4 oz. feta cheese, crumbled (125 g)
2 Tbsp. olive oil (30 ml)
2 Tbsp. balsamic vinegar (30 ml)
2 cloves garlic, peeled (6 g)
Kosher salt and pepper, to taste

Method

1. Combine together tomatoes, zucchini, basil, onion, feta cheese and garlic in a medium bowl. Drizzle with oil. Mix well. Season to taste.
2. Put the baguette slices in broiler and cook for 1-2 minutes.
3. Spoon tomato, feta and herb mixture on top of baguette.
4. Serve and enjoy.

Nutritional Information:

Energy - 161 kcal, Fat - 5.9 g, Carbs - 21.4 g, Protein - 6.0 g, Sodium - 356 mg

Veggies with Garlic Hummus

Preparation Time: 15 minutes
Total Time: 15 minutes
Yield: 16 servings

Ingredients
4 celery stalks, cut into 3-inch inches (240 g)
4 medium carrot, peeled and cut into 3-inch inches (240 g)
2 medium red bell pepper, cut into strips (240 g)

Garlic Hummus Dip
15 oz. canned chickpeas or cooked chickpeas (420 g)
4 cloves garlic, roasted and chopped (12 g)
1/4 cup olive oil (60 ml)
1/4 cup Tahini (60 g)
1/4 tsp. fresh ground pepper (0.5 g)
1/4 tsp. cumin (0.5 g)
2 Tbsp. lemon juice (30 ml)
1/4 cup reserved chickpea liquid or water (60 ml)
Kosher salt and lemon pepper, to taste

Method
1. To make the garlic hummus, first peel off all chickpea skins.
2. Put chickpeas in food processor and process for 2-3 minutes or until it has turned into a mashed consistency.
3. Add in the roasted garlic, olive oil, tahini, pepper, cumin, and lemon juice. Process for 1-2 minutes or until creamy in consistency.

4. Gradually pour in the reserved chickpea liquid and process for additional 1 minute. Season to taste.
5. Transfer hummus into a serving bowl and drizzle with olive oil.
6. Garnish with minced garlic or paprika, if desired.
7. Serve with veggie sticks on the side.

Note: Hummus is best when it is prepared before-hand and stored in the refrigerator for a couple of days before serving.

Nutritional Information:

Energy - 152 kcal, Fat - 6.4 g, Carbs - 19.2 g, Protein - 6.1 g, Sodium - 95 mg

Pita Chips and Veggies with Hummus

Preparation Time: 15 minutes
Total Time: 15 minutes
Yield: 16 servings

Ingredients

4 (2 oz. or 60 g) whole wheat pita bread, cut into 8 triangles, toasted
2 medium carrots, cut into 3-inch sticks (120 g)
4 celery stalks, cut into 3-inch sticks (240 g)

Hummus
15 oz. (420 g) canned chickpeas, drained
1/4 cup lemon juice (60 ml)
1/4 cup Tahini (60 g)
2 ½ Tbsp. water (40 ml)
1 clove garlic, minced (3 g)
3 Tbsp. olive oil (45 ml)
1 tsp. cumin, ground (2 g)
1 tsp. paprika, ground (2 g)
Kosher salt and pepper, to taste

Method

1. Make hummus by combining chickpeas, lemon juice, tahini, water, garlic, oil, cumin, and paprika in a food processor. Process for 1 minute or until mashed and has smooth texture. Season with salt and pepper, to taste. Process for another 30 seconds.

2. If the consistency of the hummus is too thick, gradually add more water into the mixture to attain the desired consistency.
3. Once the desired consistency is achieved, thoroughly scrape the hummus out of the food processor into a small serving bowl. Drizzle olive oil over the top of the mixture and garnish with paprika.
4. Serve with pita chips and veggie sticks on the side.

Nutritional Information:

Energy - 189 kcal, Fat - 6.5 g, Carbs - 26.4 g, Protein - 7.3 g, Sodium - 175 mg

Healthy Homemade Apple Chips

Preparation Time: 10 minutes
Total Time: 3 hours 10 minutes
Yield: 6 servings

Ingredients
8 (6 oz. or 180 g) medium apples
ground cinnamon, to taste

Method
1. Preheat oven to 200 F.
2. Line parchment paper over baking pan and set aside.
3. Cut apple into thin half-moon slices.
4. Arrange sliced apples in the baking pan without overlapping each other. Making sure that there is enough space in between to cook evenly.
5. Sprinkle ground cinnamon over the apples.
6. Place in the preheated oven and bake for about an hour. Then flip over the apple slices to the other side and cook for another 1 hour.
7. After cooking, turn off oven but don't take out the apple chips yet. Let it cool inside the oven for another 30 minutes to enhance crispness.
8. Serve and enjoy.

Nutritional Information:
Energy - 156 kcal, Fat - 0.5 g, Carbs - 41.4 g, Protein - 0.8 g, Sodium - 3 mg

Air-Popped Popcorn with Lemon Pepper

Preparation Time: 5 minutes
Total Time: 15 minutes
Yield: 4 servings

Ingredients
3 oz. (85 g) corn kernels, dry
lemon pepper seasoning
1 brown paper bag

Method
1. To make air-popped popcorn: put corn kernels inside brown paper bag. Fold top of brown paper bag downwards, leaving enough space to allow corn kernels to pop.
2. Place the brown paper bag with corn kernels inside the microwave oven for 1-1/2 to 2-minutes or until corn kernels stop popping after its first pop.
3. Take out popcorn, let cool for a while.
4. Open brown paper bag and sprinkle with lemon pepper seasoning.
5. After seasoning, close brown paper bag and shake the contents to evenly spread the seasoning over the popcorn.
6. Transfer into a bowl and serve.

Nutritional Information:

Energy - 11 kcal, Fat - 0.2 g, Carbs - 2.4 g, Protein - 0.4 g, Sodium - 2 mg

Homemade Baked Potato Fries

Preparation Time: 15 minutes
Total Time: 1 hour 15 minutes
Yield: 4 servings

Ingredients
4 (8 oz. or 250 g) baking potatoes
4 Tbsp. olive oil (60 ml)
1/2 tsp. paprika (1 g)
1/2 tsp. garlic powder (1 g)
1/2 tsp. chili powder (1 g)
Kosher salt and pepper, to taste

Method
1. Preheat oven to 375 F.
2. Scrub potatoes well and peel. Cut potatoes in half lengthwise then cut into sticks. Set side.
3. In a bowl, mix together olive oil, paprika, garlic powder, and chilli powder. Add the fries, and toss to coat well with olive oil.
4. In a baking pan, arrange fries in a single layer without touching each other.
5. Place inside the oven and bake for 1 hour or until brown, crispy on the outside abut tender on the inside. Flip fries every 20 minutes.
6. Once fries are baked, season with salt.
7. Serve with favourite dip on the side.

Nutritional Information:

Energy - 252 kcal, Fat - 14.3 g, Carbs - 30.0 g, Protein - 3.3 g, Sodium - 305 mg

Easy Sweet Potato Fries

Preparation Time: 10 minutes
Total Time: 45 minutes
Yield: 3 servings

Ingredients

2 large sweet potatoes, peeled (500 g)
1 ½ Tbsp. coconut oil, melted (22.5 g)
1 tsp. ground cumin (2 g)
½ tsp. ground turmeric (1 g)
¼ tsp. smoked paprika (0.5 g)
¼ tsp. ground cinnamon (0.5 g)
¼ tsp. dried sage (0.5 g)
salt and pepper

Method

1. Preheat your oven to 425 F and line a rimmed baking sheet with a piece of baking paper.
2. Cut the sweet potatoes into sticks and transfer to a medium bowl.
3. Stir in the coconut oil, seasonings, and spices. Toss the potatoes until coated with the oil and spices.
4. Arrange the sweet potato fries on your prepared baking sheet and bake for 30-35 minutes, shaking the pan halfway through cooking time.
5. Let the fries cool slightly before serving.
6. Enjoy!

Nutritional Information:

Energy - 207 kcal, Fat -7.1 g, Carbs - 34.4 g, Protein - 2.8 g, Sodium - 93 mg

Homemade Pizza Margherita

Preparation Time: 40 minutes
Total Time: 2 hours
Yield: 8 servings

Ingredients
For the Pizza dough:
1 ½ cup hot water, not boiling (375 ml)
1 ½ tsp. dry active yeast (4 g)
1 Tbsp. olive oil (15 ml)
1 Tbsp. salt (15 g)
1 Tbsp. brown sugar (15 g)
3 cups all-purpose flour (375 g)
olive oil for greasing

For the Margherita toppings:
olive oil, for brushing
4 cloves garlic, sliced thinly (12 g)
2 large tomatoes, sliced thinly (250 g)
3/4 cup mozzarella, grated (90 g)
1/4 cup parmesan, grated (30 g)
1 cup fresh basil leaves (30 g)

Method
1. To make the dough: Place hot water in a bowl and sprinkle yeast evenly over hot water. Allow the yeast to swell, about 5 minutes.
2. Stir in the olive oil, brown sugar and salt to the yeast mixture.
3. Put flour in a large bowl and add in the yeast mixture. Use a wooden spoon to stir the mixture together until combined well. During this step, the dough may turn

soft and gooey, this is natural and will make a more tender dough. Do not add flour anymore.

4. Brush some olive oil all over the bowl and also on top of the dough. Flip the dough, and brush olive oil on the other side as well.

5. Cover bowl with a clean towel and set aside in a room temperature area for 1 hour to allow dough to rise.

6. Meanwhile, in a mixing bowl, combine mozzarella and parmesan together. Set aside.

7. Wash the basil under running water to remove dirt. Arrange them in a single layer over paper towels for drying, or pat each leaf dry with paper towel.

8. Preheat your oven to 500 F.

9. Spread a generous amount of flour over a counter area and a rolling pin. Take the dough and pour flour over it as well.

10. To shape one pizza dough, roll out half the pizza dough to 3/4-inch thick, form the pizza into your desired shape (round, square or free-form).

11. Once pizza dough is ready, brush a thin layer of olive oil on top.

12. Sprinkle garlic slices over the dough, followed by placing the sliced tomatoes over the dough, leaving ¾ inches of dough untouched for the crust.

13. Sprinkle cheese mixture over toppings.

14. Using a large spatula, transfer dough onto a baking sheet or cookie sheet.

15. Place in the oven and bake for 15 minutes or until the crust turns golden brown.

16. Once done, remove pizza from oven. Spread the fresh basil leaves on top of the pizza.

17. Cut into serving pieces.
18. Serve and enjoy!

Nutritional Information:

Energy - 253 kcal, Fat - 7.1 g, Carbs - 39.7 g, Protein - 7.7 g, Sodium - 511 mg

Carrot Orange Cake

Preparation Time: 20 minutes
Total Time: 1 hour 30 minutes
Yield: 10 servings

Ingredients

1 medium seedless orange, peeled and cut into segments (140 g)
4 oz. unsalted butter, melted (125 g)
3/4 cup agave nectar (240 g)
2 (60 g) large eggs
2 medium-sized carrots, peeled and grated (120 g)
1 ½ cup cake flour (185 g)
1/2 cup almond flour (50 g)
3 tsp. baking powder (9 g)
icing sugar, to serve
cooking oil spray

Method

1. Preheat oven to 350 F.
2. Lightly grease a 22-cm baking pan with oil spray. Place a non-stick baking paper on the base and at the sides of the pan.
3. Combine orange, butter, agave nectar, and eggs in the food processor. Process ingredients until well blended.
4. Add in cake flour, almond flour, and baking powder to the mixture. Process until just combined.
5. Pour mixture in the prepared greased pan.

6. Place inside preheated oven and bake for 1 hour and 10 minutes or until a metal stick inserted at the center comes out clean. Allow to cool in wire rack.
7. When cooled, cut into squares and sprinkle with icing sugar.
8. Cut into desired slices, serve and enjoy.

Nutritional Information:

Energy - 198 kcal, Fat - 12.8 g, Carbs - 40.4 g, Protein - 4.7 g, Sodium - 91 mg

Almond Banana Bread with Flax

Preparation time: 10 minutes
Total time: 55 minutes
Yield: 10 servings

Ingredients

2 (60 g) large eggs

3/4 cup agave nectar (240 g)

1/2 stick of unsalted butter, softened (60 g)

1 cup almond flour (125 g)

1 cup buckwheat flour (125 g)

1/4 teaspoon kosher salt (1 g)

1 teaspoon baking soda (3 g)

3 mashed bananas (375 g)

1/2 cup chopped almonds (60 g)

cooking oil spray

slivered almonds, for topping

Method

1. Preheat oven to 325 F.
2. Mix together eggs, agave nectar, and butter in a large bowl.
3. Stir in almond flour, buckwheat flour, salt and baking soda until combined well.
4. Fold in mashed bananas and chopped almonds.
5. Lightly grease a loaf pan with oil spray and pour the mixture in. Sprinkle with slivered almonds on top.

6. Place pan in the oven and bake for about 45 minutes to an hour or until a toothpick inserted in the center comes out dry.
7. Transfer in wire rack and cool bread in pan for 10 minutes and then remove from the pan and let it cool completely before slicing.
8. Serve and enjoy.

Nutritional Information:

Energy - 236 kcal, Fat - 12.0 g, Carbs - 30.2 g, Protein - 5.6 g, Sodium - 195 mg

Gluten Free Banana and Walnut Bread

Preparation time: 15 minutes
Total time: 1 hour 15 minutes
Yield: 1 loaf bread

Ingredients

1 1/2 cups buckwheat flour (185 g)

1/3 cup coconut flour (35 g)

1/4 tsp. Kosher salt

1-1/2 tsp. baking powder (4.5 g)

1 tsp. baking soda (4 g)

1/2 tsp. (1 g) ground cinnamon

1/4 tsp. nutmeg, finely grated

3/4 cup walnuts, chopped (75 g)

1/3 cup coconut oil (75 g)

1/3 cup honey (115 g)

2 (60 g) whole eggs

1 cup banana, mashed (250 g)

1 tsp. vanilla extract (5 ml)

cooking oil spray

Method

1. Preheat your oven to 350°F. Grease a bread loaf pan with oil spray.
2. In a large mixing bowl, mix together buckwheat flour, coconut flour, salt, baking soda, baking powder, cinnamon and nutmeg.

3. In a separate mixing bowl, stir together coconut oil and the honey until you reach a smooth consistency. Add the eggs, banana, and vanilla. Mix well.
4. Add in the wet ingredients into the dry mixture and stir until well-combined. Fold in walnuts.
5. Pour the batter in the bread loaf pan. Place inside the oven.
6. Bake for 45-50 minutes. Check on bread occasionally and if bread top is getting a little dark, you can cover it with aluminum foil.
7. Once baking is done, remove from oven and transfer to a wire rack to let it cool before slicing.
8. Serve or store loaf in an airtight container inside the refrigerator if not eating right away.
9. Enjoy!

Nutritional Information:

Energy - 193 kcal, Fat - 11.1 g, Carbs - 21.1 g, Protein - 4.7 g, Sodium - 178 mg

Apple Cinnamon Pie

Preparation Time: 45 minutes
Total Time: 2 hours
Yield: 12 servings

Ingredients

For the Pastry:
2 cups all-purpose flour (250 g)
1 tsp. salt (5 g)
2/3 cup butter (165 g) + 2 Tbsp. (30 g)
5 Tbsp. cold water (75 ml)

For the Filling:
1/3 cup brown sugar (75 g)
1/4 cup all-purpose flour (30 g)
1/2 tsp. cinnamon, ground (1 g)
1/2 tsp. nutmeg (1 g)
1/8 tsp. iodized salt
8 (6 oz. or 180 g) medium Granny Smith apples, peeled, cored and sliced thinly
2 Tbsp. butter, unsalted (30 g)

Method

1. Make the filling by mixing flour and salt in a mixing bowl.
2. Cut in shortening by using two knives to pull through the ingredients in opposite direction until mixture becomes pea-sized.
3. Add water, one tablespoon at a time, while tossing with fork until flour is moistened evenly and pastry almost cleans the sides of the bowl thoroughly.

4. Gather pastry in a bowl and divide into two. On a lightly floured surface, shape the 2 pastry into individual flat rounds. Cover in plastic and put in refrigerator for about 45 minutes or until dough is firm and cold, yet still pliable.

5. Pre-heat oven to 425 F. Flour the rolling pin and use it to roll one pastry into rounds with 2 inches bigger than upside-down 9-inch glass pie plate. Fold the pie pastry four time. Unfold and ease into a pie plate, pressing firmly against bottom and side. Set aside.

6. In a large bowl, combine together the filling ingredients, except for the apples and butter. Gradually add the apples while stirring mixture continuously. Scoop out apple filling into the pie plate.

7. Cut butter into small cubed sized pieces and sprinkle over the filling, making sure it is evenly distributed.

8. Trim off overhanging edge of the pastry lining the pie plate.

9. Roll the remaining pastry into a 10-inch round and fold four times. Cut slits to allow steam to escape from the apple pie filling. Unfold the top pastry over filling; then trim the overhanging edge 1-inch from rim of plate. Fold and roll top edge under lower edge, pressing with fork on rim to seal the sides. Cover the edge with 2 to 3-inch strip of foil to prevent excessive browning.

10. Bake pie for 45 to 50 minutes or until crust is golden and juice of the filling bubbles through the slits of the crust. Turn off heat. Let stand for 20 minutes on wire rack.

11. Serve warm.

Nutritional Information:

Energy - 296 kcal, Fat - 13.8 g, Carbs - 42.5 g, Protein - 4.3 g, Sodium - 134 mg

Homemade Cereal and Choco Chip Cookies

Preparation Time: 10 minutes
Total Time: 25 minutes
Yield: 12 servings

Ingredients
1 cup all-purpose flour (125 g)
1/4 tsp. baking soda (1 g)
1/4 tsp. kosher salt (1.5 g)
1/3 cup unsalted butter (85 g)
2/3 cup brown sugar (150 g)
1 large egg (60 g)
1 tsp. vanilla extract (5 ml)
1-1/3 cup crispy rice cereal (40 g)
1/2 cup rolled oats (50 g)
1/2 cup dark chocolate chips (80 g)
cooking oil spray

Method
1. Preheat oven to 350 F.
2. Lightly grease two baking sheets with oil spray.
3. Combine together flour, baking soda, and salt. Mix well together and set aside.
4. Cream butter and the brown sugar until light. Gradually beat in egg and vanilla extract until well blended. Add in the flour mixture.
5. Fold in the rice cereals, oatmeal and chocolate chips.
6. Scoop out a spoonful and drop in the greased baking sheets.

7. Place in oven and bake for 10-12 minutes or until cookies are golden brown in color.
8. Remove from oven and transfer into a wire rack to cool.
9. Serve or store the cookies in an airtight container.

Nutritional Information:

Energy - 170 kcal, Fat - 7.3 g, Carbs - 24.5 g, Protein - 2.6 g, Sodium - 116 mg

Vanilla Almond Cookies

Preparation time: 10 minutes
Total time: 25 minutes
Yield: 24 servings

Ingredients

1 stick unsalted butter, softened (120 g)

2/3 cup raw sugar (150 g)

1 large egg (60 g)

2 teaspoons pure vanilla extract (10 ml)

1 cup all-purpose flour (125 g)

1/2 cup almond flour (60 g)

1/2 cup chopped almonds (60 g)

1/2 teaspoon kosher salt (2.5 g)

20 whole almonds

Method

1. Preheat your oven to 350 F.
2. Using an electric mixer, cream butter and sugar until it becomes fluffy. Add the egg, and vanilla extract.
3. Then, gradually add in the flour, almond flour, and salt.
4. Fold in chopped almonds.
5. Using a small ice cream scoop, drop the batter onto your cookie sheet lined with baking or parchment paper, about 2-inches apart. Top each with 1 whole almond
6. Bake for 12-15 minutes. Let cool in wire rack.

7. Serve and enjoy.

Nutritional Information:

Energy - 126 kcal, Fat - 8.0 g, Carbs - 12.0 g, Protein - 2.5 g, Sodium - 54 mg

Almond Crepes with Mixed Berries

Preparation time: 15 minutes
Total time: 25 minutes
Yield: 4 servings

Ingredients

1/2 cup all-purpose flour (60 g)

1/3 cup almond flour (40 g)

1 teaspoon baking powder (3 g)

1/2 teaspoon baking soda (2 g)

1/4 teaspoon of kosher salt (2.5 g)

1-1/4 cup almond milk (315 ml)

1 large egg (60 g)

2-1/2 tablespoons maple syrup (37.5 ml)

1 teaspoon almond extract (5 ml)

2 cups mixed berries (300 g)

Greek yogurt, to serve

cooking oil spray

powdered sugar

Method

1. In a large mixing bowl, combine together the all-purpose flour, almond flour, baking powder, baking soda, and kosher salt.

2. In a separate bowl, whisk together almond milk, egg, maple syrup, and almond extract.

3. Then, mix together the dry and wet ingredients until just blended. Let the batter mixture stand for about 10 minutes.
4. Heat pan over medium heat and grease with oil spray, pour about 1/4 cup of batter into the skillet. Cook both sides for about 2 minutes each side or until crepes turn golden brown.
5. Transfer into serving plates and top with some berries and a dollop of yogurt. Fold to enclose filling. Dust with some powdered sugar.
6. Serve and enjoy.

Nutritional Information:

Energy - 204 kcal, Fat - 6.4 g, Carbs - 31.7 g, Protein - 5.7 g, Sodium - 173 mg

Crispy Oatmeal Granola Raisin Bar

Preparation Time: 15 minutes
Total Time: 1 hour 5 minutes
Yield: 12 servings

Ingredients

1-2/3 cup rolled oats (166 g)
1/3 cup almond flour (35 g)
1/2 tsp. salt (2.5 g)
2 tsp. cinnamon, ground (4 g)
1 cup seedless raisins (125 g)
1 cup almonds, coarsely chopped (125 g)
1/3 cup raw honey (115 ml)
1 tsp. vanilla extract (5 ml)
1/4 cup olive oil (60 ml)
6 Tbsp. maple syrup (110 ml)
cooking oil spray

Method

1. Preheat oven to 350 degrees Fahrenheit.
2. Grease a 9"x 13" baking pan with oil spray.
3. In a mixing bowl, combine together rolled oats, almond flour, salt, cinnamon, raisins, and almonds.
4. In a separate mixing bowl, combine together raw honey, vanilla extract, olive oil and maple syrup.
5. Pour the wet ingredients onto the dry ingredients. Mix until blended well.
6. Pour granola mixture in the greased baking pan, making sure the mixture is evenly distributed on the

pan. You can use a rubber spatula to spread the mixture evenly.

7. Place inside oven and bake for 30 minutes or until edges turn golden brown.

8. Take out baking pan once cooked, and allow cooling for about 5 minutes.

9. Transfer to a wire rack and continue to cool for 15 minutes.

10. Cut into 10-12 slices.

11. Serve or store in a tightly sealed container.

Nutritional Information:

Energy - 195 kcal, Fat - 9.0 g, Carbs - 28.4 g, Protein - 2.3 g, Sodium - 100 mg

Homemade Chocolate Chip Energy Bars

Preparation Time: 4 hours 10 minutes
Total Time: 4 hours 10 minutes
Yield: 12 servings

Ingredients

1/2 cup cashews (130 g)
1 cup oats (100 g)
1/2 cup almond butter (125 g)
1 teaspoon vanilla extract (5 ml)
1/4 cup maple syrup (80 ml)
1/3 cup mini chocolate chips (55 g)

Method

1. Line your baking pan with parchment paper. In a food processor, put our cashews and oats. Pulse them together 2 times.
2. Add the wet ingredients, namely the almond butter, vanilla extract, and maple syrup. Pulse again until everything looks moist. It should form a ball shape.
3. Fold in the chocolate chips.
4. Take your mixture and your baking pan and put the mixture firmly and evenly at the bottom of the baking pan. Cover the pan and refrigerate for at least 4 to 6 hours. Once set, you can cut the slab into bars.
5. Serve and enjoy.

Nutritional Information:

Energy - 173 kcal, Fat - 10.1 g, Carbs - 16.7 g, Protein - 3.8 g, Sodium - 2 mg

Cherry Vanilla Oatmeal with Flax

Preparation Time: 5 minutes
Total Time: 20 minutes
Yield: 4 servings

Ingredients
4 cups water (1 Liter)
1 tsp. vanilla (5 ml)
1 tsp. ground cinnamon (2 g)
1/2 tsp. nutmeg (1 g)
1/4 tsp. salt (1.5 g)
1 cup whole oats (50 g)
6 oz. Greek yogurt (180 g)
1/3 cup cherry preserves (85 g)
3 Tbsp. ground flaxseeds (30 g)

Method
1. Combine water, vanilla, cinnamon, nutmeg and salt in a medium saucepan or pot. Bring to a full boil stirring mixture occasionally over high heat.
2. Stir in whole oats and flaxseeds then bring back to a boil. Lower heat and simmer for like 15 minutes.
3. While the oats are cooking, mix the Greek yogurt and cherry preserves in a small bowl and set aside.
4. Once oatmeal is cooked, add the yogurt-cherry mixture and mix thoroughly.
5. Serve and enjoy.

Nutritional Information:

Energy - 214 kcal, Fat – 8.2 g, Carbs – 26.4 g, Protein – 7.8 g, Sodium - 187 mg

Homemade Blueberry Lemon Muffin

Preparation Time: 30 minutes
Total Time: 1 hour
Yield: 12 servings

Ingredients
2 cups all-purpose flour (250 g)
1/2 cup brown sugar (110 g)
1 tsp. baking powder (3 g)
1/2 tsp. baking soda (2 g)
1/2 tsp. salt (2.5 g)
1/8 tsp. nutmeg, ground
1/4 cup butter (60 g)
1 ¼ cup low-fat buttermilk (315 ml)
1 large egg (60 ml)
1 Tbsp. lemon rind, grated (3.5 g)
1 cup blueberries (150 g)
2 Tbsp. lemon juice (30 ml)
1/2 cup powdered sugar (50 g)
cooking oil spray

Method
1. Preheat oven to 400 F.
2. In a mixing bowl, combine together flour, brown sugar, baking powder, baking soda, salt and nutmeg. Cut in butter using 2 knives until mixture is similar to a coarse meal.
3. In a separate bowl, whisk together buttermilk, egg and rind. Then add to flour mixture and mix to combine well.
4. Add the blueberries by folding it in.

5. Coat a 12-cup muffin pan with cooking spray or line with paper-liners.
6. Spoon batter into the prepared muffin pan. Place inside oven and bake for 15 minutes or until the muffins are tested done. Remove the pan from the oven and transfer each muffin onto a wire rack and let stand to cool.
7. In a mixing bowl, combine together lemon juice and powdered sugar.
8. Drizzle over muffins.
9. Serve immediately and enjoy.

Nutritional Information:

Energy - 177 kcal, Fat - 4.7 g, Carbs - 30.2 g, Protein - 3.7 g, Sodium - 92 mg

Apple Walnut and Raisin Muffin

Preparation Time: 30 minutes
Total Time: 1 hour
Yield: 12 servings

Ingredients
1-1/2 cup all-purpose flour (185 g)
1/3 cup brown sugar, firmly packed (75 g)
1 Tbsp. baking powder (9 g)
1 tsp. baking soda (4 g)
1 tsp. cinnamon, ground (2 g)
1 large egg (60 g)
1 cup skim milk or almond milk (250 ml)
1/3 cup unsweetened applesauce (85 g)
1 Tbsp. olive oil (15 ml)
1 ½ cup sultana raisins (185 g)
1 (6 oz. or 180 g) apple, finely chopped
3/4 cup (75 g) + 1/3 cup (35 g) walnuts, finely chopped

Method
1. Preheat oven to 425 F.
2. In a large bowl, mix together flour, sugar, baking powder, baking soda, and cinnamon. Set aside.
3. In a separate bowl, whisk together egg, milk, applesauce and oil until well blended. Add in raisin. Let the wet mixture stand for about 5 minutes.
4. Combine together the flour mixture and applesauce mixture. Stir well until mixture moistens. Add in apples and ¾ cup walnuts, mix well.

5. Lightly grease 12-cup muffin pan with olive oil or line muffin cups with paper liners.
6. Spoon batter and pour into each cup on the muffin pan.
7. Place inside the oven and bake for 20 minutes or until a metal stick comes out clean when inserted at the center.
8. When done baking, let muffins stand for 5 minutes to cool.
9. Transfer muffins into a wire rack, sprinkle the remaining chopped walnuts.
10. Serve and enjoy.

Nutritional Information:

Energy - 163 kcal, Fat - 8.1 g, Carbs - 20.5 g, Protein - 4.4 g, Sodium - 22 mg

Kiwi Lime Popsicles with Chia Seeds

Preparation Time: 20 minutes
Total Time: 30 minutes + 6 hours freezing time
Yield: 8 servings

Ingredients
2.2 lbs. kiwi fruit (1 kg)
1/2 cup honey (170 ml)
2 Tbsp. chia seeds (20 g)
1/3 cup lime juice (85 ml)
2 cups water (500 ml)

Method
1. Peel and cut kiwi into thin slices. Reserve about half cup. Set aside.
2. Place remaining kiwi slices, sugar, chia seeds, lime juice, and water into the blender and process until it becomes smooth.
3. Divide reserve kiwi slices in Popsicle molds or a glass cups, then pour pureed kiwi mixture. Cover and insert Popsicle stick halfway through the mixture and place in freezer. Freeze for at least 6 hours.
4. Once frozen, serve and enjoy!

Nutritional Information:
Energy - 191 kcal, Fat - 1.5 g, Carbs - 47.1 g, Protein - 2.2 g, Sodium - 6 mg

Berry Almond Popsicles

Preparation Time: 10 minutes
Total Time: 10 minutes + 4-6 hours freezing time
Yield: 8 servings

Ingredients
3 cups frozen blueberries (450 g)
1 cup unsweetened almond milk (250 ml)
1/2 cup coconut milk (125 ml)
2 Tbsp. raw honey (40 ml)
a pinch of salt

Method
1. Combine the frozen blueberries, unsweetened almond milk, coconut milk, honey, and salt to a blender. Blend until smooth.
2. Pour into popsicle molds and freeze until it becomes solid, about 4-6 hours.
3. Serve and enjoy!

Nutritional Information:
Energy - 150 kcal, Fat – 8.0 g, Carbs - 21.1 g, Protein - 1.5 g, Sodium - 190 mg

Fresh Summer Fruit Salad

Preparation Time: 10 minutes
Total Time: 10 minutes
Yield: 4 servings

Ingredients
2 (3 oz. or 85 g) medium kiwi fruits, peeled and sliced
1 cup plum, pitted and sliced (170 g)
1 cup strawberries, cleaned and halved (200 g)
1 cup raspberries (125 g)
1 cup seedless grapes (150 g)

Method
1. Place all fruits in a medium bowl. Toss to combine.
2. Divide among 4 individual serving cups.
3. Serve and enjoy!

Note: You can do this ahead of time. Cover and chill for 2 to 3 hours or until ready to serve.

Nutritional Information:
Energy - 95 kcal, Fat - 0.9 g, Carbs - 23.1 g, Protein - 1.7 g, Sodium - 3 mg

Easy Fruit Medley

Preparation Time: 10 minutes
Total Time: 10 minutes
Yield: 5 servings

Ingredients
2 (3 oz. 85 g) medium kiwifruits, peeled and sliced
1 cup strawberries, cleaned and halved (200 g)
1 cup blackberries (140 g)
1 cup blueberries (150 g)
2 cups peaches, peeled, stoned and cut into wedges (300 g)

Method
1. Place kiwi, strawberries, blackberries, blueberries, and peaches in a salad bowl. Toss to combine.
2. Divide fruit salad individual serving bowls.
3. Serve and enjoy!

Note: You can also serve this chilled with a dollop of fat-free whipped cream on top.

Nutritional Information:
Energy - 80 kcal, Fat - 0.7 g, Carbs - 19.2 g, Protein - 1.7 g, Sodium - 2 mg

Chia Pudding with Pomegranates and Almonds

Preparation time: 10 minutes
Total time: 10 minutes + 6 hours chilling time
Yield: 2 servings

Ingredients

1 cup (250 ml) almond milk, unsweetened

1/4 cup (40 g) chia seeds

6 oz. (180 g) Greek yogurt

1/4 cup (30 g) almonds, coarsely chopped

1/2 cup (90 g) pomegranate seeds

2 tsp. (14 ml) honey

Method

1. Combine milk and chia seeds in a glass bowl. Cover and keep in the fridge for at least 6-8 hours.
2. Stir in Greek yogurt. Divide this mixture among 2 serving glasses or dessert cups.
3. Top with almonds and pomegranate seeds. Drizzle with honey.
4. Serve and enjoy!

Nutritional Information:

Energy - 263 kcal, Fat - 12.1 g, Carbs - 24.2 g, Protein - 14.1 g, Sodium - 106 mg

Banana Berry and Chia Pudding

Preparation time: 5 minutes
Total time: 5 minutes + 6 hours chilling time
Yield: 4 servings

Ingredients

3 cups unsweetened almond milk (750 ml)

1 cup unsweetened coconut milk (250 ml)

1/2 cup chia seeds (80 g)

2 Tbsp. raw agave (30 ml)

2 cups fresh mixed berries, chopped

2 medium bananas, sliced (about 120 g each)

Method

1. Combine almond milk, coconut milk, and chia seeds in a glass bowl. Cover and keep in the fridge for at least 6-8 hours.
2. Stir in agave. Divide this mixture among 4 serving glasses or dessert cups.
3. Top with mixed berries and banana slices. Serve and enjoy!

Nutritional Information:

Energy - 238 kcal, Fat – 14.0 g, Carbs - 28.2 g, Protein - 3.7 g, Sodium - 83 mg

Granola Yogurt and Strawberry Parfait

Preparation time: 5 minutes
Total time: 10 minutes
Yield: 4 servings

Ingredients

2-½ cups low-fat vanilla yogurt (375 g)

2 cups granola (100 g)

2 cups fresh strawberries, sliced (400 g)

1/2 cup dry roasted almonds, coarsely chopped (60 g)

4 tsp. honey (30 ml)

Method

1. Equally divide yogurt among 4 cups or small parfait glasses.
2. Then, add granola, almonds, and strawberries.
3. Finally, drizzle each with a teaspoon of honey.
4. Cover and chill the parfait for at least an hour before serving.
5. Enjoy!

Nutritional Information:

Energy - 310 kcal, Fat - 10.9 g, Carbs - 41.0 g, Protein - 12.6 g, Sodium - 100 mg

Granola Choco and Berry Parfait

Preparation Time: 15 minutes
Total Time: 15 minutes
Yield: 4 servings

Ingredients

1 cup strawberries, fresh, sliced (200 g)
1 cup blueberries (150 g)
1 cup vanilla-flavored Greek yogurt (250 g)
1 cup granola (50 g)
2 oz. (60 g) dark chocolate, cut into small pieces

Method

1. In 4 cups or parfait glasses, alternately layer the granola, Greek yogurt, berries, and dark chocolate.
2. Serve and enjoy.

Note: You can chill this before serving for best results.

Nutritional Information:

Energy - 198 kcal, Fat - 12.9 g, Carbs - 38.0 g, Protein - 12.1 g, Sodium - 63 mg

Yogurt Corn Flakes and Berry Parfait

Preparation Time: 15 minutes
Total Time: 15 minutes
Yield: 4 servings

Ingredients
2 cups low-fat yogurt, vanilla (500 g)
1 cup corn flakes (30 g)
4 Tbsp. raspberry syrup (60 g)
1 cup raspberry, fresh (125 g)
1 cup blackberries, fresh (140 g)

Method
1. In 4 round glasses or parfait glasses, layer the bottom with yogurt and then followed by the raspberry syrup.
2. Add in crushed corn flakes and berries.
3. Top with another layer of yogurt, cereals, and berries. Cover the parfait and place in the fridge for at least an hour.
4. Serve and enjoy.

Nutritional Information:
Energy - 161 kcal, Fat - 1.9 g, Carbs - 26.1 g, Protein - 8.3 g, Sodium - 153 mg

Vanilla Yogurt and Blackberry Delight

Preparation Time: 10 minutes
Total Time: 15 minutes + 6 hours chilling time
Yield: 4 servings

Ingredients
2 cups vanilla-flavored Greek Yogurt (500 g)

Compote:
2 cups blackberries (280 g)
3 Tbsp. maple syrup (60 ml)
2 Tbsp. water (30 ml)

Method
1. In a pan over low heat, place blackberries, caster sugar and water. Bring to a simmer until fruit begins to burst.
2. Pour half of blackberry compote mixture in a blender and process until smooth.
3. Mix together puree and the remaining blackberry mixture. Cover and place in the refrigerator for an hour or until ready to serve.
4. Upon serving, divide yogurt among 4 ramekins or dessert cups and top with prepared blackberry sauce.
5. Serve immediately and enjoy.

Nutritional Information:
Energy - 150 kcal, Fat - 1.9 g, Carbs - 21.5 g, Protein - 12.5 g, Sodium - 52 mg

Vanilla Almond Panna Cotta with Mango

Preparation Time: 15 minutes
Total Time: 20 minutes
Yield: 6 servings

Ingredients

2 (7 g) envelopes unflavored gelatin
1 3/4 cups almond milk (440 ml)
3/4 cup half-and-half (185 ml)
1/2 cup agave nectar (160 ml)
1 teaspoon pure vanilla extract (5 ml)
2 cups fresh ripe mangos, diced (330 g)

Method

1. In a small bowl, pour 1/3 cup almond milk and then sprinkle gelatine powder. Let stand for 4 minutes.
2. In a medium saucepan over medium heat, combine together 1-1/3 cup almond milk, half and half, sugar, and vanilla extract. Bring to a simmer for 2-3 minutes. Remove from heat.
3. Pour in gelatine mixture, stir ingredients together until gelatine dissolves and evenly distributed.
4. Pour mixture in ramekins. Cover and chill for at least 6 to 8 hours.
5. Upon serving, top panna cotta with diced mangoes.
6. Serve and enjoy.

Nutritional Information:

Energy - 198 kcal, Fat - 4.6 g, Carbs - 39.7 g, Protein - 2.8 g, Sodium - 55 mg

Almond Panna Cotta with Strawberry Puree

Preparation Time: 15 minutes
Total Time: 15 minutes + 6 hours chilling time
Yield: 6 servings

Ingredients

2 Tbsp. unflavored gelatin powder (14 g)
1 cup half and half cream (250 ml)
1/3 cup agave nectar (110 ml)
2 tsp. vanilla extract (10 ml)
2 cups almond milk (500 ml)
1 lb. frozen strawberries, halved (450 g)
1/3 cup honey (115 ml)
cooking oil spray

Method

1. In a small saucepan, pour 2 tablespoon of cream and sprinkle gelatine on top. Let the gelatine stand for 5 minutes. Turn on stove, heat saucepan over medium-low heat, stir the mixture together until gelatine dissolves completely and is evenly distributed.
2. In a separate saucepan over medium heat, combine together remaining cream, agave nectar and vanilla. Stir together until mixture is steaming. Remove from heat.
3. Stir in gelatine mixture and whisk in almond milk.
4. Lightly spray cooking oil on ramekins. Pour panna cotta mixture on greased ramekins, cover with cling

film, and then store in refrigerator for 6 hours up to 2 days.

5. Make the strawberry sauce by placing frozen strawberries and honey in a food processor and processing until strawberries become pureed.

6. Upon serving, take out panna cotta from the refrigerator. Run knife within ramekin edges and turn over panna cotta on a serving plate. Drizzle with strawberry puree and the top with fresh strawberries.

7. Serve and enjoy.

Nutritional Information:

Energy - 210 kcal, Fat - 5.7 g, Carbs - 39.6 g, Protein - 2.8 g, Sodium - 68 mg

Homemade Raspberry Yogurt

Preparation Time: 5 minutes
Total Time: 10 minutes
Yield: 4 servings

Ingredients

1 cup fresh raspberries (125 g)
4 (6 oz. or 180 g) Greek yogurt, plain
2 Tbsp. sugar-free raspberry syrup (30 ml)
1/2 tsp. pure vanilla extract (2.5 ml)
mint sprigs, for garnish

Method

1. In a small bowl, whisk together yogurt, raspberry syrup and vanilla extract. Cover and chill in fridge for an hour or until ready to serve.
2. Divide yogurt mixture in 4 individual serving cups or small bowls. Top with fresh raspberries and garnish with mint sprig.
3. Serve and enjoy.

Nutritional Information:

Energy - 137 kcal, Fat - 2.5 g, Carbs - 10.5 g, Protein - 17.6 g, Sodium - 75 mg

Blueberry Yogurt with Flax

Preparation Time: 5 minutes
Total Time: 5 minutes
Yield: 4 servings

Ingredients
1 ½ cup frozen blueberries (225 g)
4 (6 oz. or 180 g) low-fat yogurt
2 Tbsp. lemon juice (30 ml)
2 Tbsp. honey (40 ml)
2 Tbsp. flaxseeds (20 g)
mint sprigs, for garnish

Method
1. In a food processor, combine half of the blueberries, yogurt, lemon juice, honey, and flaxseeds.
2. Divide yogurt mixture into serving cups.
3. Garnish with remaining blueberries.
4. Serve and enjoy.

Nutritional Information:
Energy - 204 kcal, Fat - 3.4 g, Carbs - 29.7 g, Protein - 10.8 g, Sodium - 122 mg

Strawberry Cereal and Yogurt Drink

Preparation Time: 5 minutes
Total Time: 5 minutes
Yield: 4 servings

Ingredients

1 cup Greek yogurt (250 g)
2 cups frozen strawberries, sliced thinly (440 g)
2 Tbsp. rolled oats (15 g)
1 Tbsp. strawberry syrup (15 ml)
1 ½ cup skim milk (375 ml)
2 Tbsp. wheat germ (15 g)

Method

1. In a blender, combine yogurt, frozen strawberries, rolled oats, strawberry syrup, and skim milk. Process until smooth and creamy.
2. Pour in 2 serving glasses.
3. Top with sliced strawberries and sprinkle with wheat germ.
4. Serve and enjoy.

Nutritional Information:

Energy - 133 kcal, Fat - 1.5 g, Carbs - 19.0 g, Protein - 10.6 g, Sodium - 75 mg

Orange Tofu and Cinnamon Smoothie

Preparation Time: 5 minutes
Total Time: 5 minutes
Yield: 3 servings

Ingredients

1 cup Mandarin orange segments (200 g)
8 oz. silken tofu (250 g)
1 cup soy milk (250 ml)
1/2 tsp. ground cinnamon + additional for topping (1 g)
10 ice cubes
orange rind, sliced thinly for garnish

Method

1. Combine orange, tofu, soy milk, cinnamon, and ice in a blender. Process until smooth.
2. Pour smoothie into 3 chilled glasses.
3. Sprinkle with ground cinnamon and top with sliced orange zest.
4. Serve and enjoy.

Nutritional Information:

Energy - 158 kcal, Fat - 4.6 g, Carbs - 19.3 g, Protein - 10.8 g, Sodium - 100 mg

Yogurt Strawberry and Pistachio Dessert

Preparation time: 10 minutes
Total time: 10 minutes
Yield: 2 servings

Ingredients

1 cup Greek yogurt (250 g)
1 cup fresh strawberries, hulled and quartered (200 g)
1/4 cup pistachios, chopped (30 g)
2 tsp. honey (15 ml)

Method

1. Divide yogurt in 2 small serving bowls or dessert cups.
2. Top with fresh strawberries and pistachios.
3. Drizzle with honey. Cover and chill in fridge for an hour or until ready to serve.
4. Enjoy!

Nutritional Information:

Energy - 160 kcal, Fat - 5.7 g, Carbs - 17.3 g, Protein - 12.1 g, Sodium - 74 mg

Banana Cinnamon Smoothie

Preparation Time: 5 minutes
Total Time: 5 minutes
Yield: 2 servings

Ingredients

2 cups almond milk, unsweetened (500 ml)
2 small bananas, sliced (200 g)
1/2 tsp. (1 g) ground cinnamon + additional for topping
6 ice cubes

Method

1. Combine together almond milk, banana, cinnamon, and ice cubes in a blender. Process until smooth and creamy, about 30 to 45 seconds.
2. Pour smoothie into 2 chilled glasses. Sprinkle with ground cinnamon.
3. Serve and enjoy.

Nutritional Information:

Energy - 121 kcal, Fat - 2.8 g, Carbs - 24.5 g, Protein - 2.1 g, Sodium - 151 mg

Apricot Peach and Carrot Cooler

Preparation Time: 5 minutes
Total Time: 5 minutes
Yield: 2 servings

Ingredients

8 oz. fresh apricots (250 g)
1 medium peach (150 g)
1 medium carrot, peeled and sliced (60 g)
2 Tbsp. lemon juice (30 ml)
1 cup cold water
4 ice cubes

Method

1. Remove and discard stones from peach and apricots. Peel and cut into small pieces.
2. Place the fruits and carrot slices in a high-speed blender and process until ingredients are pureed. Add lemon juice, water, and ice cubes. Blend again until smooth.
3. Pour in glasses. Garnish with a slice of apricot or peach.
4. Serve and enjoy!

Nutritional Information:

Energy - 73 kcal, Fat - 0.8 g, Carbs - 16.5 g, Protein - 1.9 g, Sodium - 18 mg

Choco Almond Protein Shake

Preparation Time: 5 minutes
Total Time: 5 minutes
Yield: 2 servings

Ingredients
1 cup almond milk, unsweetened (250 ml)
2 scoops whey protein powder, chocolate flavor (80 g)
1 cup water (250 g)
1/2 tsp. vanilla extract (2.5 ml)
6 ice cubes
dark chocolate, shaved

Method
1. In a blender, combine almond milk, soy protein powder, water, vanilla extract, and crushed ice. Process ingredients until smooth.
2. Pour into 2 chilled glasses. Sprinkle with chocolate shavings.
3. Serve and enjoy!

Nutritional Information:
Energy - 138 kcal, Fat - 3.1 g, Carbs - 4.3 g, Protein - 22.6 g, Sodium - 134 mg

Beet Apple and Ginger Smoothie

Preparation Time: 5 minutes
Total Time: 5 minutes
Yield: 3 servings

Ingredients
4 beets, peeled and cut into quarters (340 g)
1 large apple, peeled, cored and cut into quarters (180 g)
1 tsp. fresh ginger, grated (3.5 g)
1 medium carrot, sliced (60 g)
1 ½ cup water (375 ml)
6 ice cubes

Method
1. Combine beets, apple, ginger, carrot, water, and crushed ice in a high-speed blender. Process until smooth.
2. Pour in 3 chilled glasses. Garnish with mint and a slice of beetroot and ginger, if desired.
3. Serve and enjoy!

Nutritional Information:
Energy - 108 kcal, Fat - 0.3 g, Carbs - 19.3 g, Protein - 1.5 g, Sodium - 66 mg

Pineapple Lychee Smoothie with Hemp Seeds

Preparation Time: 5 minutes
Total Time: 5 minutes
Yield: 2 servings

Ingredients
1 cup pineapple, cut into cubes (250 g)
3/4 cup lychees, peeled and pitted (145 g)
2 tsp. hemp seeds (7 g)
2 tsp. honey, optional (14 ml)
1 cup water (250 ml)
6 ice cubes

Method
1. In a high-speed blender, combine together pineapple, lychees, hemp seeds, honey, water, and ice. Process for 1 minute or until smooth.
2. Pour smoothie into 2 chilled glasses. Garnish with lychee or a chunk of pineapple, if desired.
3. Serve and enjoy.

Nutritional Information:
Energy - 100 kcal, Fat - 1.0 g, Carbs - 23.6 g, Protein - 1.2 g, Sodium - 2 mg

Orange Carrot and Ginger Juice

Preparation Time: 5 minutes
Total Time: 5 minutes
Yield: 2 servings

Ingredients
2 medium orange, cut into small pieces (280 g)
2 medium carrot, cut into small pieces (120 g)
1/4 lemon (25 g)
1-inch fresh ginger (5 g)
ice cubes, to serve

Method
1. Process oranges, carrots, lemon and ginger in a juicer.
2. Pour into 2 chilled glasses over ice cubes.
3. Serve and enjoy.

Nutritional Information:
Energy - 119 kcal, Fat - 0.3 g, Carbs - 29.7 g, Protein - 2.5 g, Sodium - 43 mg

Pineapple Kiwi and Coconut Pleasure

Preparation Time: 5 minutes
Total Time: 5 minutes
Yield: 2 servings

Ingredients
2 cups pineapple chunks (500 g)
2 medium kiwi, cut into small pieces (170 g)
1 mint sprig (2 g)
1 cup coconut water (250 ml)
4 ice cubes

Method
1. Place pineapple, kiwi, mint, coconut water, and ice cubes in a high-speed blender. Process until mixture becomes smooth.
2. Pour into 2 chilled glasses over ice cubes.
3. Serve and enjoy!

Nutritional Information:
Energy - 128 kcal, Fat - 0.6 g, Carbs - 32.8 g, Protein - 1.8 g, Sodium - 4 mg

Watermelon and Strawberry Surprise

Preparation Time: 5 minutes
Total Time: 5 minutes
Yield: 2 servings

Ingredients

2 cups fresh watermelon, cubed (300 g)
1 cup fresh strawberries, halved (200 g)
1 cup coconut water (250 ml)
6 ice cubes

Method

1. In a blender, combine watermelon, strawberries, coconut water, and ice cubes.
2. Pour smoothie into 2 chilled glasses. Garnish with a slice of watermelon or strawberry, if desired.
3. Serve and enjoy!

Nutritional Information:

Energy - 92 kcal, Fat - 0.7 g, Carbs - 21.4 g, Protein - 2.2 g, Sodium - 129 mg

Orange Banana and Goji Berry Smoothie

Preparation time: 5 minutes
Total time: 5 minutes
Yield: 2 servings

Ingredients

1 seedless orange, peeled and cut into segments (140 g)

1 medium banana, sliced (120 g)

2 Tbsp. dried goji berries (15 g)

1 cup coconut water (250 ml)

2 Tbsp. chia seeds (20 g)

2 Tbsp. lime juice (30 ml)

6 ice cubes

Method

1. In a high-speed blender, add in oranges, banana, goji berries, coconut water, and ice. Blend until smooth.
2. Pour in 2 chilled glasses. Garnish with a slice of orange or lime if desired.
3. Serve and enjoy!

Nutritional Information:

Energy - 176 kcal, Fat - 2.6 g, Carbs - 38.1 g, Protein - 3.4 g, Sodium - 128 mg

Berry Banana and Almond Smoothie

Preparation Time: 5 minutes
Total Time: 5 minutes
Yield: 2 servings

Ingredients
2 small bananas, peeled and sliced (200 g)
1 cup frozen strawberries, halved (200 g)
1 cup almond milk, unsweetened (250 ml)
2 Tbsp. wheat germ (15 g)

Method
1. In a blender, combine together bananas, frozen strawberries, almond milk, and wheat germ. Process until smooth.
2. Pour into 2 chilled tall glasses. Garnish with strawberry, if desired.
3. Serve and enjoy.

Nutritional Information:
Energy - 155 kcal, Fat - 2.6 g, Carbs - 32.6 g, Protein - 4.1 g, Sodium - 77 mg

Pear Orange and Carrot Juice

Preparation Time: 10 minutes
Total Time: 15 minutes
Yield: 2 servings

Ingredients
1 medium pear, cut into small pieces (180 g)
2 medium oranges, cut into small pieces (280 g)
1 medium carrot, cut into small pieces (60 g)
ice cubes, to serve

Method
1. Place the pear, oranges, and carrot in a juice extractor.
2. Pour juice into 2 serving glasses over ice cubes.
3. Serve and enjoy.

Nutritional Information:

Energy - 114 kcal, Fat - 0.3 g, Carbs - 29.0 g, Protein - 1.7 g, Sodium - 22 mg

Peach Tea and Mint Cooler

Preparation Time: 5 minutes
Total Time: 5 minutes
Yield: 4 servings

Ingredients
3 cups freshly brewed tea (750 ml)
1 cup peach nectar (250 ml)
few mint leaves
2 Tbsp. honey (40 ml)
ice cubes, to serve
peach slices, to serve

Method
1. Combine tea, peach nectar, mint, and honey in a pitcher. Stir.
2. Pour in tall glasses with ice cubes and peach slices. Garnish with mint sprig, if desired.
3. Serve immediately and enjoy.

Nutritional Information:
Energy - 67 kcal, Fat - 0.0 g, Carbs - 17.4 g, Protein - 0.2 g, Sodium - 0 mg

Chilled Strawberry Infused Water

Preparation Time: 5 minutes
Total Time: 5 minutes
Yield: 2 servings

Ingredients
2 cups water (500 ml)
1 cup fresh strawberries, hulled and quartered (200 g)
ice cubes, to serve

Method
1. Divide strawberries in 2 glass jars with lid. Fill with water. Cover and store in refrigerator overnight.
2. Add ice before serving.
3. Serve and enjoy.

Nutritional Information:
Energy - 23 kcal, Fat - 0.2 g, Carbs - 5.5 g, Protein - 0.5 g, Sodium - 1 mg

Ginger Lemon Tea with Honey

Preparation Time: 5 minutes
Total Time: 15 minutes
Yield: 4 servings

Ingredients

4 cups (1 L) water
1 oz. (28 g) fresh ginger root, thinly sliced
1/4 cup (60 ml) lemon juice
2 Tbsp. (40 ml) honey

Method

1. In a saucepan, combine water and ginger. Bring to a boil. Reduce heat and simmer for 10-15 minutes. Pour in a tea pot.
2. Stir in lemon juice and honey.
3. Pour tea mixture into four serving cups.
4. Serve immediately and enjoy.

Nutritional Information:

Energy - 38 kcal, Fat - 0.1 g, Carbs - 9.6 g, Protein - 0.2 g, Sodium - 9 mg

Hot Masala Chai

Preparation Time: 5 minutes
Total Time: 5 minutes
Yield: 4 servings

Ingredients

3 cups (750 ml) water
1 cup (250 ml) skim milk
1 star anise
1 Tbsp. (2 g) black tea leaves
2 Tbsp. (40 ml) agave nectar
1 tsp. (2 g) cardamom, ground
4 small cinnamon sticks, to serve

Method

1. In a saucepan, combine water, star anise, and agave nectar. Bring to a boil. Add milk and cook until heated through. Remove from heat. Pour into a tea pot and let sit for 3 minutes.
2. Stir in black tea leaves. Steep for 3-5 minutes.
3. Pour tea mixture into four serving cups. Sprinkle with cardamom.
4. Serve with cinnamon stick and enjoy.

Nutritional Information:

Energy - 58 kcal, Fat - 0.1 g, Carbs - 12.2 g, Protein - 2.2 g, Sodium - 38 mg

Malted Choco Cappuccino

Preparation Time: 5 minutes
Total Time: 5 minutes
Yield: 1 serving

Ingredients

3/4 cup (185 ml) skim milk
1 shot (30 ml) espresso
1 Tbsp. (7 g) chocolate malt powder
1/4 tsp. cinnamon, ground

Method

1. Heat the milk on the stove until it almost reaches a boil. Whisk briskly with a wire whisk to make foam.
2. In a serving glass or cup, mix together espresso, chocolate malt powder, and cinnamon.
3. Pour milk and foam.
4. Serve immediately and enjoy.

Nutritional Information:

Energy - 156 kcal, Fat - 1.0 g, Carbs - 27.7 g, Protein - 7.1 g, Sodium - 142 mg

Sweet Almond Coffee

Preparation Time: 5 minutes
Total Time: 5 minutes
Yield: 1 serving

Ingredients
3/4 cup (185 ml) hot water
1 shot (30 ml) espresso
1 oz. (30 ml) almond milk
1/4 tsp. almond extract
1 tsp. (5 g) brown sugar

Method
1. In a serving cup, stir together hot water, espresso, almond milk, almond extract, and brown sugar.
2. Serve immediately and enjoy.

Nutritional Information:
Energy - 22 kcal, Fat - 0.3 g, Carbs - 4.6 g, Protein - 0.2 g, Sodium - 29 mg

Thanks a lot for reading!

I hope you enjoyed reading and making all the recipes here.

For more great tasting recipes, please check out all my published books on Amazon.